REVISED EDITION

Playing the Market

Karen Isaacson

Dale Seymour Publications®
Parsippany, New Jersey

This book is published by Dale Seymour Publications®, an imprint of
Addison Wesley Longman, Inc.

Dale Seymour Publications
299 Jefferson Road
Parsippany, New Jersey 07054-0480
Customer Service: 800-872-1100

Managing Editor: Catherine Anderson
Senior Editor: John Nelson
Project Editor: Jeri Hayes
Production/Manufacturing Director: Janet Yearian
Production/Manufacturing Coordinators: Roxanne Knoll, Mark Pierce
Design Director: Phyills Aycock
Design Manager: Jeff Kelly
Text and Cover Design: Don Taka

This Book Is Printed
On Recycled Paper

Order number 21909
ISBN 0-7690-0106-8

2 3 4 5 6 7 8 9 10–ML–03 02 01 00

CONTENTS

Using This Unit

Introduction v

Materials vi

Teacher's Role vii

Skills and Assessment ix

Extensions x

Using the Internet xiii

Unit Lessons

Lesson 1: Reading the Stock Market Pages 1

Lesson 2: Introducing the Simulation 5

Lesson 3: Stock Purchasing Decisions 11

Lesson 4: Reporting and Calculating Commissions 13

Lesson 5: Purchasing Stock 17

Lesson 6: Monitoring Profits and Losses 19

Lesson 7: Selling Stock 22

Lesson 8: Wrapping Up the Unit 23

Appendix

Assessment Tools

Rubric for Portfolios 27

Rubric for Oral Reports 28

Rubric for Journals 29

CONTENTS

Teacher Observation Sheet (BLM) 30

Self-Evaluation (BLM) 31

Group Evaluation (BLM) 32

Blackline Master Worksheets

Reading the NYSE 33

Converting Fractions to Decimals 36

Simulation Guidelines 37

Job Descriptions 38

Purchase Request 39

Checkbook Register 40

Checks 41

Broker's Commission Report 42

Order to Sell 43

Track Record 44

Glossary 45

Parent Letter 47

Samples of Filled-In Investment Forms

Purchase Request Sample 48

Checkbook Register Sample 49

Check Samples 50

Broker's Commission Report Sample 51

Order to Sell Sample 52

Track Record Sample 53

This unit is your guide to using the Stock Exchange Composite Transactions to simulate having your students invest money in the stock market and then follow the progress of those investments. The daily lessons are easy to understand and easy to teach even if you know little or nothing about the stock market or about investing. Your students will work in cooperative learning groups to complete the activities, and these groups will engage in friendly competition to see which of them can make the most money in the stock market.

You'll want to take some time to read through Lessons 1 and 2, in particular, to aquaint yourself with basic information on presenting this unit and on reading the stock market pages.

Time Considerations

In approximately seven 40-minute class periods your students can be prepared to read and understand the stock market listings, learn the simulation guidelines, form their learning groups (or "investment companies"), and purchase their stocks. After these initial lessons, the amount of class time you choose to devote to having students monitor their investments, construct graphs, and so on, is flexible. You may decide to allow fifteen minutes several times each week and then assign the graph constructions as in-class work or as homework. To get a good feel for watching the stock market, the simulation should run for six to eight weeks but can run the entire school year. The time necessary for the final activity depends on what elements you decide to assign. There are several suggestions in Lesson 8: Wrapping Up the Unit.

Finding It Easy

This book introduces basic stock market terminology and includes a reproducible glossary (pages 45–46). You will find that the glossary gives the definition for the context in which the word is used here, not for all its possible meanings. Besides the glossary, you will find blackline masters and sample investment forms in the Appendix. You may want to check your teacher resource center and local libraries for additional resources.

A guide to Using the Internet (pages xiii–xiv) will help your students use the World Wide Web to find information about companies in which they may want to invest, and will teach them how to get stock quotes on-line.

In Short

Your students will be buying and selling stock in order to earn as much money as possible. As in real life, they may lose quite a bit of money! As their broker, you are the person from whom they will be buying and selling. Please read pages vii–viii for detailed information on your role. The extension activities on pages x–xii are designed to encourage your students to teach themselves, and each other, more about the marketplace. While it is not a comprehensive list, the Extensions will provide enrichment opportunities for your students during the course of the simulation.

MATERIALS

Most of the materials required for the stock market simulation are provided as blackline masters in the Appendix of this book.

You will need the financial section of newspapers that publish stock exchange transactions. If you wish, you may contact the *Wall Street Journal* Education Office to ask about a classroom subscription. Their toll-free phone number is (800) 568-7625.

The other materials you will likely have around your classroom. Most of the materials can be assembled and photocopied before beginning the unit.

For the Entire Class

- Several current copies of the *Wall Street Journal,* or another newspaper that publishes stock exchange transactions
- An overhead transparency of each blackline master
- An overhead projector/screen

One Copy for Each Student

- Blackline Masters: Converting Fractions to Decimals, Self-Evaluation, Group Evaluation (see Appendix)

One Copy for Each Group

- Blackline Masters: Simulation Guidelines, Job Descriptions, Checkbook Register, Broker's Commission Report

Several Copies for Each Group

- Blackline Masters: Checks, Order to Sell, Track Record
- Tagboard, cardboard, construction paper (approx. 22" × 28"), or manila folders
- Graph paper
- Colored pencils, pens, or crayons
- Several lengths of butcher paper for classroom charts
- Calculators (one per student, if possible)

You can teach this unit knowing little or nothing about the stock market from the outset and learn along with your students. Or, you can enrich the unit by adding personal knowledge and historical information.

Customizing the Unit

During the course of this simulation, you will act as both the stockbroker and the bank auditor. You will find as you go through this material that you can customize the unit to suit your preferences by adding extra activities (see Extensions, pages x–xii), or by eliminating some steps.

This unit is planned for use with cooperative learning groups. However, the unit can easily be adapted for individual student work. (Note that if you are preparing materials for individual study, you'll need to prepare per-group items for each individual.) The Simulation Guidelines will need to be modified to indicate an individual's responsibilities rather than a group's responsibilities. If students are working individually, you will not be using the Assigning Jobs section of Lesson 4, nor will you use the Blackline Master: Job Descriptions.

For Younger Students

If you would like to modify this unit for younger students, leave out the steps involving the broker's commission. Students make more money with this method, but will be more likely to buy and sell randomly. If you decide to leave out the broker's commission, you may want to place a limit on how often investment companies can replace existing stocks with new ones. To further simplify the simulation, you can have students stick with their first purchasing decisions and not allow them to sell until the last day of the simulation.

Opening Your Own Brokerage House

In the sample paperwork found in the Appendix, the ficticious stock brokerage is named "Acme Brokerage House," but you can choose any name suited to you and your classroom. When students are buying stocks and paying your broker's commission, they will be making their checks payable to the brokerage company name you have chosen.

As the Stockbroker

You may decide to copy a set of checks for yourself. If so, it's a good idea to photocopy them on a different colored paper than you use for the investment company (student) checks. You can use your checks to "pay" investment companies when they are selling stocks back to the brokerage firm. If you want to avoid the extra step of filling out checks payable to the investment companies, you may simply record the transactions as a deposits in the companies' checkbook registers.

The broker also needs to carefully review stock Purchase Requests and Track Records to make sure students are keeping accurate records. If students are making mistakes, or not keeping records, they will not be able to construct graphs or to properly complete other activities in the unit. There is a place on the Purchase Request form for your "stamp of approval" before it is placed into the investment company portfolio. Any rubber stamp (or your initials) can be used.

As the Bank Auditor

You will cancel checks as necessary and distribute the canceled checks back to the investment companies. Any rubber stamp can also be used as your bank stamp. The auditor should meet with each investment company periodically, especially toward the beginning of the project, to review the portfolio organization and recordkeeping.

Your last job as auditor will be to assign the final activity to your investment companies. You will find a number of suggestions in Lesson 8: Wrapping Up the Unit, and you will be able to decide which of the items you would like your students to complete.

SKILLS AND ASSESSMENT

There are a number of skills your students will be utilizing while playing the market. This simulation can be used as a vehicle for teaching any of these skills, or it can be used as a follow-up. Ideally, this will help reinforce the real-world applications of the math skills students have been learning in the classroom.

- Organizing information
- Graphing
- Converting fractions to decimals
- Basic accounting and recordkeeping
- Decision making
- Cooperating within a group
- Adding, subtracting, and multiplying decimal numbers
- Finding percents
- Reading stock market pages
- Using the Internet to conduct research
- Calculator skills
- Presenting information in written and oral forms
- Self-evaluation

There are a number of assessment suggestions included with this unit. You will find a table of contents for rubrics and evaluation forms (blackline masters) on page 26. The assessment tools are designed to be flexible so that they can be used even as you become familiar with this unit (by repeated use) and customize the lessons and assigned activities to your personal preferences. The Blackline Master: Teacher Observation Sheet, can be used any time students are working. The notes you make on completed Observation Sheets can be used if you wish to consult with an individual student. (Student conferences are not part of any of the lessons, but, of course, as teachers we often find ourselves discussing student achievement, progress, or behavior on an individual basis.)

Observation Sheets can also be used if you have particular students whom you wish to document regarding their ability to accomplish a particular task, communicate effectively, or organize their work. You might decide to observe all of the members of one investment company on one day, another company the next time, and so forth. Once you have gathered the observations, the rubrics you have used, and the self- and group evaluations, you will be well equipped to give students one overall grade for the entire unit if that is what you wish to do. Each teacher presenting this unit can decide which assessment tools to use and which to set aside.

EXTENSIONS

In this section, you'll find several social studies, history, and language arts extensions for this unit. Depending on your students' abilities with fractions, decimals, percents, and calculator skills, you may decide to develop additional math extensions or remediations.

- Have your students keep a journal throughout the unit. You may choose to have all students do the written work, or you may assign the task to the Operations Manager, and have other group members give input. Each day your class works on this project, write a journal topic on the board. Following are some suggested topics.

  What did your group accomplish today? What steps must you still take before you have purchased your stock?

  Explain how to find the cost of one share of stock x.

  How did your group go about deciding which stocks to purchase?

  What problems did you encounter when figuring out how many shares of each stock to buy? How did you solve those problems?

  What is a broker's commission? Explain how to calculate a broker's commission.

  For what reasons might you choose to sell the shares in one of your companies? Describe the steps involved in selling stock.

  You have been assigned to research information about one of the companies in which you have invested. How do you plan to go about this research?

- Create a class stock index, similar in style to the Dow Jones. This can be done as a class project, or done in small groups. Help students choose ten high-profile companies to use as indicators. Each day, or several times each week, the closing prices of these ten companies should be recorded and the profits or losses calculated. Take an average of these profits and losses to determine how many points (dollars) the stock market has gone up or down. Compare this average to the average group investments.

Note: *The Dow Jones, begun in the 1880s, was originally an average of 11 stocks, chosen by Charles Henry Dow. Today, the Dow is no longer an actual average but is calculated by a rather complicated process.*

- Research the history of the Dow Jones Index.
- Have each group send for a prospectus of one of the companies in which they've invested. See Using the Internet, page xiii, for details.

- Arrange to visit a brokerage house or the stock exchange. If this is impractical in your location, invite a stockbroker to address your students. Following are some sample questions to ask your visiting broker.

  When did you first become interested in the stock market?

  How much education and what kind of training does it take to become a stockbroker?

  How much time do you spend doing research each day? What do you do during a typical workday?

  How would you recommend going about deciding which stocks to buy?

  How do you go about researching a company in which you want to buy stock?

  What's the best stock you've ever bought?

  What factors can influence you to sell your shares of a particular stock?

  Why are all those people shouting and raising their hands at the stock exchange?

  Why do people buy stock through a broker rather than directly from the company? (Or) Why do people buy stock from the stock exchange rather than directly from the company?

  What is your favorite investment website?

  Can you recommend books or publications about the stock market that you've found interesting?

- Research the 1929 stock market crash. Report on the reasons for and consequences of the crash.
- Have students bring in current events on the marketplace.
- Check your teacher resource center or library for videos on the stock market.
- If your students are ready, extend the Converting Fractions to Decimals assignment (see Blackline Master, page 36), and have them combine dividing decimals, changing decimals to percents and rounding. Let students try the following calculator activity.

  Have students calculate figures for the Percent Yield column. The Percent Yield *is calculated by* dividing *the* Dividend *by the* Close. *Take a look at a stock table. Give students any dividend amount and the closing price. Students should perform the division using a calculator. The decimal answer must then be changed to a percent by multiplying by 100. The last step is to round to the nearest tenth of a percent. Student answers can easily be checked by comparison to the newspaper.*

- If you subscribe to the Classroom Edition of the *Wall Street Journal,* the Teacher's Guide is full of support material, including discussion topics, quick questions, analytical questions, and homework suggestions to use in conjunction with each issue of the paper.
- Are there any big companies based in the town or city where your school is located? What are they? Do they sell stock publicly? If your town has a local newspaper with a business section, it may have a special listing for local companies with stock offerings.
- Stock market simulation games, in which you can enroll students, are occasionally advertised in journals and newspapers. Some of these programs have enrollment fees, while others do not. The games usually run eight to ten weeks and may offer prizes and/or free newspaper delivery. Keep a lookout in your newspaper for these opportunities, if you're interested.

USING THE INTERNET

Computers can be used for this simulation in three ways. First, students can go on-line to find the closing prices of their stocks. Next, they can use the Internet to reseach information about a specific company. Finally, students can go on-line to search for general information about the stock market. Lesson plans, classroom and field trip activities, and market information is readily available on the Internet, and is constantly increasing. In fact, you'll want to be careful to discriminate between what's worth your time and what isn't. Websites are continually in a state of change, and there are always new sites being added. Following is a selection of sites, organized by category, that you may find helpful.

Finding Stock Quotes

The New York, American, regional stock exchanges, and NASDAQ (National Association of Securities Dealers Automated Quotation) all have their own websites.

http://www.nyse.com

This address will take you to the New York Stock Exchange home page. This is an extremely valuable site for stock quotes and company information. On the home page you can click on the "Stock Prices" button. Selecting "Stock Prices" will take you to a page that will ask you what you wish to search for. The default setting will have you select by symbol. However, if you click and hold on "Symbol," you have the option to select by "Company Name Containing the Word . . . ." By using one of these two options, symbol or company name, your students should be able to locate the stock they are interested in, if it is traded on the NYSE.

When the NYSE Closing Prices and Corporate Profile page comes up for the company you have selected, you can find information on the closing price, on that company's industry, on the original date the stock was listed on the exchange, on the high, low, volume, and number of shares outstanding, and other corporate information. In some cases, you will be able to scroll to the bottom of the activity screen and find a link to the company home page. The company home page will usually provide you and your students with all kinds of additional information. This is an ideal place for students to begin research for their final reports.

An annoying roadblock you may encounter while searching stock exchange websites is the message, "No documents found." For your students' purposes, the most efficient response to this problem is to choose a different company whose documentation is accessible and up-to-date.

http://www.amex.com

This website opens with the option to go live to the Amex trading floor. It also shows the five most active stocks on the exchange for the day, and, via the Fast Quote button, will give you quotes from the NYSE and NASDAQ. If you select the "Listed Companies" link, you can look up investments within categories: All Companies, Information/Technology, Healthcare, Financial, Industrial, or Natural Resources.

http://www.nasdaq.com

The NASDAQ home page is great for checking several quotes in one quick stop. Here, you can enter ten symbols at a time to get quotes from NASDAQ, NYSE, and Amex. If you don't know the company symbol, there is a "Symbol Look-Up" option. The SiteNews section offers the latest news directly related to NASDAQ.

Some regional exchange website addresses are:

Pacific Stock Exchange	**http://www.pacificex.com**
Chicago Stock Exchange	**http://www.chicagostockex.com**
Boston Stock Exchange	**http://www.bostonstock.com**
Philadelphia Stock Exchange	**http://www.phlx.com/index.stm**
Kansas City Board of Trade	**http://www.kcbt.com**

Finding Information About a Selected Company

Nearly everyone and everything seems to have a website these days. Once your students have settled on a particular company, you might have them try an Internet search by typing in <http://www.companyname.com>. Very often, this general search strategy will yield positive results.

Another site students like to visit is the financial network at <http://www.cnnfn.com>. This website provides access to stock charts, corporate profiles, and company snapshots. There is a "competitors" link which offers information about companies in the same line of business. The news link will search for news articles written about the company you have selected. It's an interesting place to roam around. You might also investigate <http://www.quicken.com>. Here you can get stock quotes and company information, including phone numbers and business descriptions.

Kiplinger Online at <http://www.kiplinger.com> is a great site for teachers and parents. Kiplinger offers business forecasts and personal financial advice, but of particular interest to students and teachers is the Kids & Money link. It's definitely worth visiting.

LESSON 1

Reading the Stock Market Pages

In this lesson, students will

- **learn and practice how to extract from a newspaper a stock's name, its current price, and its net change**
- **convert fractions to decimals and round to the nearest hundredth**

Approximate Time
30–50 minutes

Materials
- Newspapers that list stock market transactions
- Calculators (one per student, if possible)
- Blackline Master: Reading the NYSE (1 per student)

The Stock Tables

Key to this unit is being able to read the stock tables. It's really not difficult to extract the necessary information from the tables to complete the activities. The first task is to decide which newspaper(s) your students will use. Different newspapers list the stock table information with small variations. To save the cost of your subscribing to a newspaper for your students, you might consider finding out which newspapers students have delivered to their homes. Ask students to bring in the financial section each day.

The *Wall Street Journal* provides the most comprehensive stock tables and is widely available. The *Wall Street Journal* also offers a Classroom Edition especially for high school students. While the Classroom Edition doesn't publish the stock exchange transactions, it has interesting articles about investing, technology, careers, and so forth. It also has full-color graphics and comes with a teacher's guide. If you have high school students, it's well worth looking into. For information, call (800) 544-0522 or check the website at <http://info.wsj.com/classroom>.

Once you have selected a newspaper, direct students to open to the stock market pages and locate the boxed area that describes how to interpret the listings. It will be titled, for example, "Explanatory Notes," or "How To Read the Stock Tables." This information should tell you how many companies are listed and should identify the segment of the market those companies represent. For example, the *San Francisco Examiner* lists the 2,900 most-active issues on the New York Stock Exchange. The *Examiner* also has listings for Amex (American Stock Exchange) and NASDAQ. If you would like more detailed information than what is provided in this book, contact individual stock brokerages or the *Wall Street Journal;* they have booklets available upon request.

In this lesson, students will learn to extract three pieces of information from the stock tables: the stock name, the last closing price, and the net change.

The Stock Name

In most newspapers, the stock market pages list an abbreviation for a company's full name. The abbreviated names are usually found under the heading "Stock." In addition to its abbreviated name, each stock also has a unique symbol. The symbol is used to identify the stock on electronic systems, databases, and the stock exchange ticker. For example, the full name of one company on the NYSE is Hershey Food Corporation. Both the *San Francisco Examiner* and *USA Today* list the company as "Hershey." The stock symbol for the Hershey Corporation (not given in either newspaper) is "HSY." The symbol is useful when looking up the stock on the Internet.

The full company name, rather than the abbreviated form, is good to have if students are going to research a specific company. Students may want to find out how long a company has been in business, what products or services they offer, how many people they employ, where the company is headquartered, its corporate mission statement, and so on. This information can be included in the students' final reports. It may also be helpful when students are deciding which stocks to purchase. For example, if investors find out a company or corporation is involved in the manufacturing and sales of cigarettes, they may decide to invest their money elsewhere. For suggestions on how to look on-line for information about a company, please refer to Using the Internet, pages xiii–xiv.

The stock type is indicated by abbreviations immediately following the company symbol, for example, "pf," "wt," "rt," "un," or "wi." The abbreviations pertain to such things as distribution of dividends, rights to buy at certain prices and in certain amounts, whether the stock must be bought as a "package deal," and so on. There are many other abbreviations contained in the stock data tables; refer to the information box in your newspaper for a complete listing.

If no abbreviations appear after the company symbol, the stock is referred to as "common." It's generally a good idea for students to limit their choices to common stocks. This will avoid the problem of your having to learn in depth all of the details associated with different kinds of stock. If you are a veteran stock market participant, you may wish to allow your students more flexibility in their choices.

The Stock Price

The stock price is the amount of money per share the stock was selling for when the exchange closed on the previous day. When investors choose new stocks to buy, they turn to this column to find out how much they will have to pay. When investors want to sell stock, this column tells them how much per share they can expect to be paid.

Again, different newspapers display the prices in different formats. The *Press Democrat* and the *San Francisco Examiner* list the closing prices under the heading "Last." The amount is given as a mixed number, a whole number with a fraction. The *San Francisco Chronicle* also uses the heading "Last," but uses decimals rather than mixed numbers. The *Wall Street Journal* uses the heading "Close," with mixed numbers.

How Much Money Is 1/8?

One reason people find the stock exchange pages hard to interpret is that cents usually are presented as fractions. For your classroom simulation, you may decide whether your investors are going to round off the eighths of a dollar, or if they are going to calculate the price out to the thousandths place. Will 1/8 = $ .125 or $ .13? (Note: The sample calculations in this book use rounded-off numbers.) If you will be using a newspaper that gives the price of shares as a mixed number, have students take out a calculator and practice converting some mixed numbers to decimals.

Converting Fractions

On the chalkboard, write the fraction *1/8*. Instruct students to enter the equation: *1 divided by 8 equals* into their calculators. The display should read 0.125. Round to the nearest hundredth and place a dollar sign in front. Ask, "How much money does this number stand for?" Give as much practice at this as necessary, depending on your students' ability.

Once students get used to seeing dollar amounts represented without a dollar sign, and with fractions instead of decimals, understanding the stock pages will become much easier. Also, on the Blackline Master: Converting Fractions to Decimals, students will chart fraction-to-decimal equivalents and can refer back to the chart, if necessary, when reading over the stock exchange figures.

Net Change

Net change is calculated by subtracting the currently listed closing price from the previous day's closing price. If the stock value has risen since the day before, a plus sign (+) will appear before the dollar amount (frequently shown as a fraction of a dollar). If the stock closed at a lower price, a minus sign (–) will appear. If there is no entry in the net change column, then there has been no change from the previous day. If the listing is in boldface, it means the close is either up or down more than 5% from the day before.

At first, have students concentrate on learning the Stock, Close (or Last), and Net Change columns. Students will use the data in these columns to complete their investigations into the stock market.

Provide Some Practice

Once you have reviewed the Stock, Close, and Net Change columns, distribute a newspaper to each pair of students. Everyone should open to the same page of the same newspaper. Ask the following questions:

What is the name of this newspaper? The date?

On which exchange are these stocks traded? (NYSE, NASDAQ, Amex)

Find the stock abbreviation PepsiCo. What do you think it stands for?

What was this stock selling for at the close of the last business day?

Is this stock up or down from the last business day?

What is the net change for this stock?

Quiz your students on several stocks until you're sure they've understood how to locate and interpret the data.

Tell students that they will next be assigned to investment groups. Explain that they will be given a certain amount to invest and that you will show them how to use information in the stock tables to make investment decisions.

Give students a copy of the Blackline Master: Reading the NYSE. This information can be kept as a reference if students wish to refresh their memories on the stock, close, and net change column headings. Students can also use Reading the NYSE to gain information on the other columns of information included in the stock tables. As an option, you may decide instead to have students clip out "Explanatory Notes" or "How to Read the Stock Tables" directly from the newspaper.

LESSON 2

Introducing the Project

In this lesson, students will

- **join an investment group**
- **review the rules of the stock market simulation**
- **choose stocks to purchase**
- **learn how to manipulate the number of shares to arrive near (but not exceed) the target amount of $4,900**
- **receive some background information on the stock market (optional)**

Approximate Time

40–60 minutes

Materials

- Calculators
- Newspapers
- Scratch paper

Background Information

The amount of class time needed for this lesson depends on how deeply you want to explore the history of the market. It will help to give a brief history of the stock market to generate student enthusiasm for the project. Lesson 1 began with students opening up a newspaper and getting acquainted with the stock tables. This lesson takes a step back once students have become interested and enthusiastic about the subject. The unit is organized this way in order to "hook" students' attention before delving into a historical discussion. This unit does not offer comprehensive historical information for the teacher or the student for two reasons. First, the unit is designed to be easily taught by any teacher, even if he or she knows little or nothing about the stock market. Therefore, there is no lesson in which the teacher stands before the students and delivers a lengthy "history of the stock market" speech. Secondly, the instructional plan for this unit calls for students to choose a subject on which to conduct a research project, and to present the information to the entire class. If for example, students are studying U.S. history, research projects can be assigned on finding information about the 1920s, the stock market crash, and the Great Depression. Begin a discussion to find out what students already know about the stock market and how it works. If you decide to teach the unit as a straightforward simulation, a simple review of the simulation guidelines and a general discussion about the market can be completed in about 40 minutes. The following is for your information, and it is up to you how much you would like to relate to your students.

Why Stock? What Is It?

Issuing stock is one way that a corporation can raise money. Another possible method for a corporation to raise money is to borrow it from a bank. A bank loan, however, comes with the requirement for the corporation to pay back the borrowed money at specific times in specific amounts. On the other hand, if a corporation offers stock for sale, they do not have to reimburse the buyers in the same manner. Instead, companies pay their stockholders a share in the profits; these payments are called *dividends*. If there are no profits, dividends will not likely be paid. This payment arrangement is an advantage to raising money by issuing stock.

Once a person has bought stock (or shares) in a corporation, that person becomes a *shareholder* or *stockholder*, which means he or she shares in the ownership of the company. Shareholders can vote at meetings. The number of shares owned determines how many votes a person gets. This would probably be considered a disadvantage of offering stock by the original owners of the company.

A corporation cannot just decide to set a price, and start selling stock. They first must get permission to sell stock from a federal agency called the Securities and Exchange Commission. The Securities and Exchange Commission has stringent requirements that must be met before they will authorize a corporation to begin selling stock.

When you buy stock you are buying a piece of the ownership of a company. Stocks rise and fall in value according to how much new buyers are willing to pay and how low current owners are willing to sell.

The Stock Exchanges

The New York Stock Exchange is also sometimes called The Big Board. It is the oldest and the largest of the exchanges. An exchange is a place where stocks are bought and sold. The function of the exchange, aside from providing a place for buyers and sellers to come together, is to keep an eye on everyone to ensure fair play. This may include making sure everyone keeps good records and that trades are all done publicly. Secret trading is not allowed.

The New York Stock Exchange began along with the first banks of our country. To have banks, you need to have people ready to invest capital (start-up money). People were willing to invest by buying shares (stock) in the new banks, but they also needed a system for later selling their shares. They needed a place of exchange. A small group of men began to buy and sell these bank shares for themselves, and for other people they represented in New York, at a place on Wall Street. This informal buying and selling eventually became the New York Stock Exchange.

Differences Between the Exchanges

The New York Stock Exchange lists the largest and most stable companies. The American Stock Exchange tends to list more medium-sized companies. The regional exchanges include the Pacific Stock Exchange, located both in San Francisco and Los Angeles, the Chicago Stock Exchange, the Philadelphia Stock Exchange, the Boston Stock Exchange, and the Cincinnati Stock Exchange. These exchanges list local companies not on the NYSE or Amex, as well as some larger companies that may list on both the regional and major exchanges.

NASDAQ stands for National Association of Securities Dealers Automated Quotation. NASDAQ is not an exchange; there is no actual building where these stocks are traded. NASDAQ was created in 1971 as an electronic listing exclusively for over-the-counter stocks. Over-the-counter stocks are smaller stocks that are commonly traded but are not listed on any of the exchanges. NASDAQ essentially is a listing of unlisted stocks. In March, 1998, however, the governing board of NASDAQ and Amex announced a merger. The headline of the news release on the NASDAQ home page dated March 18, 1998 read, "NASDAQ and Amex to Combine to Create a Global Market of Markets." The effects of this merger on the world market have yet to be assessed. As with stock market news in general, however, you can depend on this adage: "Just when you think you know what's going on, watch out, because it's going to change."

The amount of background information you choose to provide your students is flexible. If time permits, have your students do some research and teach each other about the history of the stock market. Please refer to Extensions, page x, for some project ideas. This unit can be taught from a mathematics approach, or from a combination of math, history, language arts, and social studies.

The Game Is Afoot

Explain that each student will become part of an investment group that will attempt to make as much profit as possible by playing the stock market and competing against other investment groups to see which one can earn the most money.

This simulation is set up as a contest to see who in your classroom can make the most money by investing in the stock market. No actual play money changes hands (as in Monopoly, for example); instead, transactions are made by writing checks and are recorded in student checkbook registers. It is fun for the students if a tangible prize if offered as an incentive for the most successful investors. You may also consider the idea of a tangible prize for the investment group exhibiting the best teamwork.

The simulation guidelines are meant to be flexible. If you have younger students, you may opt to lower the $5,000 investment limit to $1,000 and lower the commission rate from 2% to .4%.

Forming Companies

For younger students, the simulation seems to work best by forming "investment companies." These companies will work as cooperative groups throughout the remainder of the unit. With older students, you may decide to have the activities performed on an individual basis or in pairs. (This method *does* make more work for the broker!) Please refer back to Teacher's Role, page vii, if you decide to go with individual investors rather than groups.

To encourage balance and diversity, assign students to cooperative learning groups rather than letting them choose their own groups. When forming the groups, try to put a leader, an above-average student, an average student, and one who may need extra encouragement in each group. If your class does not divide evenly by four, groups of three will work better than groups of five.

Once students are seated in their investment groups and the rules of the stock market simulation have been explained, you can demonstrate how to go about choosing stocks and how to calculate how many shares to buy from each company to spend approximately $4,900.

Begin by asking students, "Can you name some companies I might want to invest in?" Invariably, students suggest large corporations with which

Simulation Guidelines

1. Each group will receive $5,000.00 to invest in the stock market.
2. Investors must spend a minimum of $4,900.00 on stocks and broker's commissions but may not exceed the $5,000.00 limit. Leftover funds will be kept in the investment company checking account for possible later use. (It probably won't be possible for investors to reach the exact $5,000.00 amount.)
3. Each group must choose at least three but no more than five companies from which to purchase stock.
4. A 2% commission must be paid to the stockbroker for every stock bought and for every stock sold.
5. Every group is responsible for keeping a Track Record for each stock it owns. This record, and all other stock records, will be kept in the investment portfolio.
6. Periodically, the total profit or loss will be recorded onto a master economic data sheet. (See Lesson 6: Monitoring Profits and Losses.)
7. A final activity will be completed by all investment groups as assigned. (Final activity suggestions are explained in Lesson 8: Wrapping Up the Unit.)

they are familiar. Usually, fast food chains, supermarkets, soft drink giants, and sports shoe manufacturers are the first choices.

List the ideas on the chalkboard and then turn to the newspaper stock market listings to try to locate the stock abbreviations for the companies your students suggested. You can usually guess from its abbreviation the full name of a big corporation.

Student suggestions often include such well-known companies as Safeway, Reebok, Pepsi, and Boeing. Check the newspaper stock market pages to be sure you can locate the data for these companies. Then draw a chart on the chalkboard that resembles the one below.

Company	**Closing Price**	×	**Number of Shares**	=	**Amount Spent**
Safeway	66 7/16				
Reebok	26 11/16				
PepsiCo	36 1/8				
Boeing	47 5/8				

Next, engage students by saying, "Let's pretend that these are the companies that my investment group would like to invest in. How do we figure out how many shares of each we should buy?"

"Let's see if we can experiment with the figures and come up with a total of approximately $4,900."

"How many Safeway shares should we buy?"

Write down whatever is suggested and begin to fill in the chart. For example, students may suggest 10 shares of Safeway, 5 shares of Reebok, 15 shares of Pepsi, and 1 share of Boeing. (Generally, younger students begin by estimating way too few!)

Fill out the chart with whatever your students suggest. It will now look like the example on page 10.

Company	Closing Price	×	Number of Shares	=	Amount Spent
Safeway	66 7/16	×	10	=	664.40
Reebok	26 11/16	×	5	=	133.45
PepsiCo	36 1/8	×	15	=	541.95
Boeing	47 5/8	×	1	=	47.63
					$1,387.43

If your students have calculators, ask them to do the multiplication for you.

Ask, "Have we spent all of the money in our budget?" (In this case, no.)

"What should we do in order to get closer to our $4,900 target amount?"

Students will probably figure out that they need to adjust and readjust the number of shares until they are within range. You can do the adjusting on the board for the entire class, or let the groups manipulate the figures. This activity takes a lot of work with the calculator and scratch paper.

To make sure everyone finds a solution to this activity, ask one or two groups to report what worked for them by recording their solutions on the board. A final sample that works might look like this:

Company	Closing Price	×	Number of Shares	=	Amount Spent
Safeway	66 7/16	×	25	=	1,661.00
Reebok	26 11/16	×	36	=	960.84
PepsiCo	36 1/8	×	31	=	1,120.03
Boeing	47 5/8	×	24	=	1,143.12
					$4,884.99

Having a total figure of $4,884.99 will work nicely because when you add in the 2% broker's commission ($97.70) you will end up with a grand total of $4,982.69. This is close to the $5,000 limit but does not exceed it.

LESSON 3

Stock Purchasing Decisions

In this lesson, students will

- **choose names for their investment groups**
- **choose three to five companies from which to buy stock**
- **calculate how many shares of each stock to buy**

Approximate Time

120 minutes, or two math periods

Materials

- Calculators
- Newspapers (1 financial section per group)
- Scratch paper

Choosing Companies to Invest In

Students should be seated with their investment groups and provided with current stock market listings, calculators, and lots of scratch paper. Remind students of the simulation guidelines, and instruct them to go ahead and make decisions with their group on which companies to buy stock in and how much to invest.

At this point, the class generally falls unusually quiet, and thirty pairs of eyes focus on the teacher.

"Is it better to invest in three, four, or five companies?" someone usually asks. (It all depends on the individual stocks and how they perform. There is no definitive answer.) Students often solve this dilemma by allowing each member of the investment company to choose one stock.

"How do we know which stocks will go up?" is the next question. (You don't!)

"You mean we just guess?" (Yes! Unless you've gotten some hot stock tips from a reliable source, or have gotten a flash of insight from keeping up with the latest financial news publications—guess.)

Sixth graders generally have no problem figuring out which companies to invest in. They peruse the stock tables until they see a familiar abbreviation and choose accordingly. Popular choices include Disney, Microsoft, Reebok, Hershey, and Nike.

Sometimes an investment group will choose a company based on the stock abbreviations with the most unusual combination of letters. After the fact, students might ask the teacher to reveal the company's full name! For an idea of how to get information about a company when you have only its abbreviation, please refer to Using the Internet, page xiii.

Students often find this next step of the simulation to be a lot of fun. Give them time to search through the stock tables for a company that catches their attention. When students make their stock choices, it is very important that they record the name of the stock listing from which they made their selection. (NYSE, NASDAQ, or Amex). This will save time and aggravation later on. In order to look up the stock on the Internet, they will also need this information. To simplify the selection process, you may decide to use only the NYSE.

Once a company has been selected for investment, students must write down the company name, stock symbol, and closing price, just as they practiced in Lesson 3. They will need to manipulate the number of shares to buy until they reach the $4,900 target figure.

Have students save this information, as they will need it for Lesson 4.

Reporting and Calculating Commissions

In this lesson, students will

- design a portfolio to hold checks, a checkbook register, and other paperwork
- select investors to take on specific responsibilities within the investment groups
- learn to calculate 2% of a number
- construct a chart to display purchasing decisions
- report orally to the class

Approximate Time
60 minutes

Materials
- Blackline Master: Job Descriptions (1 per group)
- Tagboard, cardboard, a manila envelope, or construction paper (1 piece per group)
- Chart paper (1 piece per group)
- Marking pens
- Calculators

Designing a Portfolio

Each group needs to design a portfolio to hold all of its paperwork. A piece of tagboard measuring 22" × 28", scored and folded in half, is a perfect size. Holes can be punched at the top open edge and a string tied through to complete the portfolio. If tagboard is too expensive or unavailable, a large piece of construction paper or cardboard will work. You can also simply use a manila folder to contain the paperwork. Finally, supply each group with two envelopes—one to contain blank checks, the other for canceled checks.

Investment Company Names

While students put together their portfolios, they should decide on names for their investment companies. The company name should be featured on the portfolio. Students should be given a day for this task because the decision often generates more debate and serious discussion than deciding which stocks to buy.

Assigning Jobs

Each student should be assigned a specific job within his or her investment company. If there are only three students in a company, or on days when a student is absent, someone will have to double up on responsibilities. All participants in an investment company decide together which stocks to purchase.

Emphasize to students that the company jobs must be taken seriously. The group members are there to help one another. Remind students that they will also be grading one another's performance at the end of the unit. This can be a good opportunity to reward teamwork with a prize or some other special recognition for an investment group or for an individual. You may consider using information you have written down on the Blackline Master: Teacher Observation Sheet, to help you in making a decision about which individuals in which groups have been particularly successful in accomplishing a task, demonstrating organizational skills, and communicating effectively.

Every member in an investment company participates in deciding which stocks to buy and when they should be sold. The Operations Manager leads group meetings, but decision making within the group should be democratic.

Job descriptions should be kept in the portfolio to remind students of their individual responsibilities to their group.

Job Descriptions

Purchasing Agent Responsible for filling out all paperwork regarding the buying and selling of stocks, including Purchase Requests, Order to Sell forms, and Track Records.

Runner Responsible for out-of-seat duties, such as taking Stock Purchase Requests to the broker, recording information on the classroom economic data sheets, and picking up supplies. The runner also supervises the construction of graphs showing profits and losses.

Accountant Checks all of the math figures made by the Purchasing Agent, and keeps track of broker's commissions. The accountant also manages the account, and writes and signs checks.

Operations Manager Keeps the Track Records (explained in Lesson 7), and organizes the portfolio. The Operations Manager is also responsible for leading the group meetings.

Reporting to the Class

During the last math period, students should have come up with purchasing decisions totaling approximately $4,900. They may still have some adjusting and readjusting to do. While students are finalizing their calculations, draw a skeleton of a report chart on the chalkboard. It should look something like this:

(Group Name)

Stock Abbr.	Price per Share	×	# of shares	=	Cost	+	2% of Cost	=	Total

Calculating the Broker's Commission

If students don't know how to find 2% of a number, show them how to perform this calculation. With a calculator and a few minutes of instruction and practice, students should be able to master the skill.

Remind students that you are the stockbroker; you will be buying and selling stock for their investment companies. You will need to be paid for your services. The next time the investment companies meet, they will each be provided a checking account with a $5,000 balance. They will have to write two checks to you: a check for your broker's commission and a check for stock purchases.

Company Reports

Give each group a piece of butcher paper on which to present their investment decisions. A final chart may look something like this:

Stock-Co

Dakota
Ashley
Rachel
Travis

New York Stock Exchange

	Stock Name	Price	# of Shares	Total Price	2% Commission
1.	Nike	$41.75	24	$1,002.00	$20.04
2.	Hershey	$63.81	26	$1,659.06	$33.18
3.	Texaco	$53.69	20	$1,073.80	$21.48
4.	Bank of America	$72.69	15	+ $1,090.35	$21.81
				$4,825.21	

Total of Commission = $96.51

Grand Total = $4,921.72

When the charts are complete, have each investment group report to the class on what they have decided to buy and why. They should also identify their company's name and explain why it was chosen. Check for mathematical accuracy on their charts.

Hang the charts around your classroom. They will provide students with a visual reminder of the buy-in price of their stocks and the broker's commission. This will be helpful when they are ready to write checks and fill in the Order to Buy forms.

LESSON 5

Purchasing Stock

In this lesson, students will

- **fill out checks and begin a checkbook register**
- **fill out a Purchase Request**
- **enter a commission payment on the Broker's Commission Report**

Approximate Time
90 minutes

Materials
- Calculators
- Blackline Masters
  - Purchase Request (several copies per group)
  - Checkbook Register (one per group)
  - Broker's Commission Report (one per group)
- Overhead Transparencies
  - Purchase Request
  - Checks
  - Checkbook Register
  - Broker's Commission Report

Managing the Checking Account

Each group's accountant should receive a Checkbook Register, showing a $5,000 balance, and a packet of checks. Use the overhead projector to review the correct method for filling out checks and recording debits, credits, and the balance in a checkbook register. (See pages 40 and 41.) Explain that accountants will have to correctly fill out checks in order to purchase their group's stocks. The checks will then have to be submitted to you, the stockbroker, along with a completed Purchase Request form.

Purchase Requests/Broker's Commissions

Again using the overhead projector, show students step-by-step the correct method for filling out a Purchase Request and a Broker's Commission Report. (See pages 39 and 42.) Their stocks have already been chosen. Even though the figures they are working with are a few days old now, don't worry about it. Have students use the figures they have on their report charts from Lesson 5. If the charts are posted on your classroom walls, students can easily look at their charts to find the information they will need.

Filling out the Purchase Requests, the checks, the Checkbook Register, and the Broker's Commission Report can take quite awhile, depending on your students' abilities.

The Purchase Requests, Broker's Commission Report, and Checkbook Register need to be kept in the investors' portfolio. The packet of checks can be kept in an envelope attached to the inside of the portfolio.

Buying Stock

When the Purchase Request has been filled out, checks (payable to the broker) must be written for the stock and for each commission amount. When all of the paperwork is complete, the runner delivers the paperwork to the broker for approval.

The balance of the $5,000 not spent on stocks and commissions today is left in the investment company's checking account. For example, if total stocks plus commissions comes to $4,987.58, then the checking account would show a balance of $12.42. Students may get a chance later to invest this money.

The Auditor

Once students are satisfied with their choices and have invested all of their money, the Purchase Request forms have to be carefully audited. Each company will submit three to five purchase requests and two checks—one for the total of the purchase requests and one for the total amount due to the broker for commissions. As bank auditor, you will need to verify their figures and add up the check amounts to make sure each company has spent the required amounts. If you have checked the figures on the charts, these should already be correct. Also make sure that each company has filled out a Broker's Commission Report.

When you are satisfied that each company has successfully completed this very important phase of the unit, stamp your approval on the Purchase Request forms, cancel the checks, and hand everything back to the investment companies.

Your students are now all set to track the progress of their stocks.

LESSON 6 Monitoring Profits and Losses

In this lesson, students will

- check and record the closing prices of their stocks × number of times
- construct a line graph
- construct a master economic data chart
- report orally to the class

Approximate Time
This phase of the unit takes 20–30 minutes each time you have students check their stocks. Once they have checked their stocks 6–8 times over a period of weeks, they will have gathered enough information to construct graphs.

Materials
- Several current copies of the *Wall Street Journal* or another newspaper that prints the stock tables
- Graph paper
- Colored pencils, pens, or crayons
- Calculators
- Butcher paper or chart paper
- Blackline Master: Track Record (several copies per group)
- Overhead Transparency: Track Record

Tracking Stock

The investment companies will need one Track Record sheet for each company in which they have purchased stocks. They will need a new Track Record sheet for each day you have them check the progress of their investments, so it's a good idea to have a stack of them on hand. Students should check their stocks once a week. It's a good idea to change the color of the Track Record sheets each week. This really helps students when they are organizing their paperwork.

Track Records need to be kept updated (by the Operations Manager) and in careful order in the portfolio. It is from these Track Records that students will pull information to construct their graphs.

Demonstrate on the overhead projector the correct way to fill out a Track Record; then have students try it on their own. When the work is checked and initialed by the accountant, it's a good idea for you to review all of the paperwork.

If the progress of the stocks is not monitored correctly, students will not be able to complete the activities in the unit successfully.

Using Track Records to Construct Graphs

Once students have compiled information on their stocks, they can construct a line graph for each stock to show its performance over time.

Review line graphs with students, making sure they remember to label each graph properly.

A Graphing Device

A simple mnemonic device, created by a middle school teacher, can help your students complete their graphs. The acronym RUTAL, read, "Are you tall?" reminds students of the features that they should include in their line graphs. You may want to post the RUTAL reminder on the chalkboard. (See Sidebar.)

Students can write RUTAL on the side of their graphs and then check off each letter as a self-monitoring tool.

R = Readability

Is the graph neat, clean and easy to read?

U = Units

Are the units you have chosen for your axis marked at regular intervals?

T = Title

Does your graph have a title?

Does it describe the graph's data?

A = Axis

Axes should be marked *x* and *y*.

L = Labels

Both the *x*- and *y*-axis need to be labeled appropriately.

In this case, the *x*-axis will probably be "date" and the *y*-axis will be "closing price in dollars."

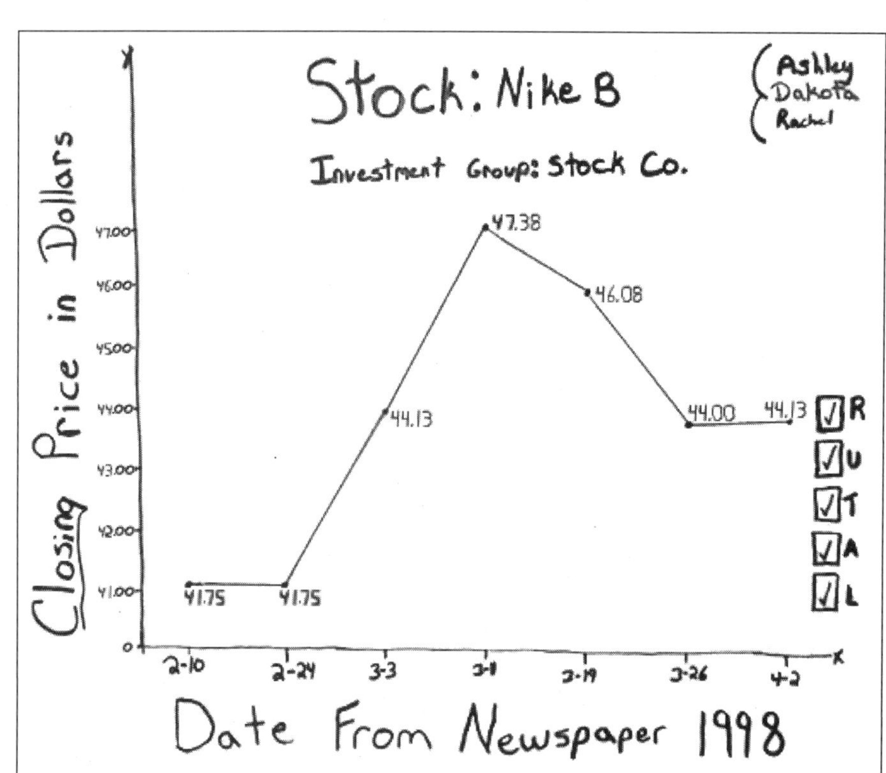

Master Economic Data Sheet

Since this simulation is also a contest, it will help students to know how they are doing from time to time compared to the other investment groups. Plan several times during this unit to have companies tally up their total profits or losses to date and to report that information to the rest of the class on a master economic data sheet.

Calculating Profit and Loss

Set a date for progress reports. On that day, the investment companies will check the closing price of each of their stocks. Students will have to compare their original purchase price with the new close, and subtract to find out how much they would earn or lose if they were to sell all of their stocks. Next, chart this profit or loss on the class master economic data sheet, along with the profits or losses of all other stocks. Then add up the three to five figures (the number of companies in which stocks are owned) to arrive at a total profit or loss figure. The data sheet will look something like this:

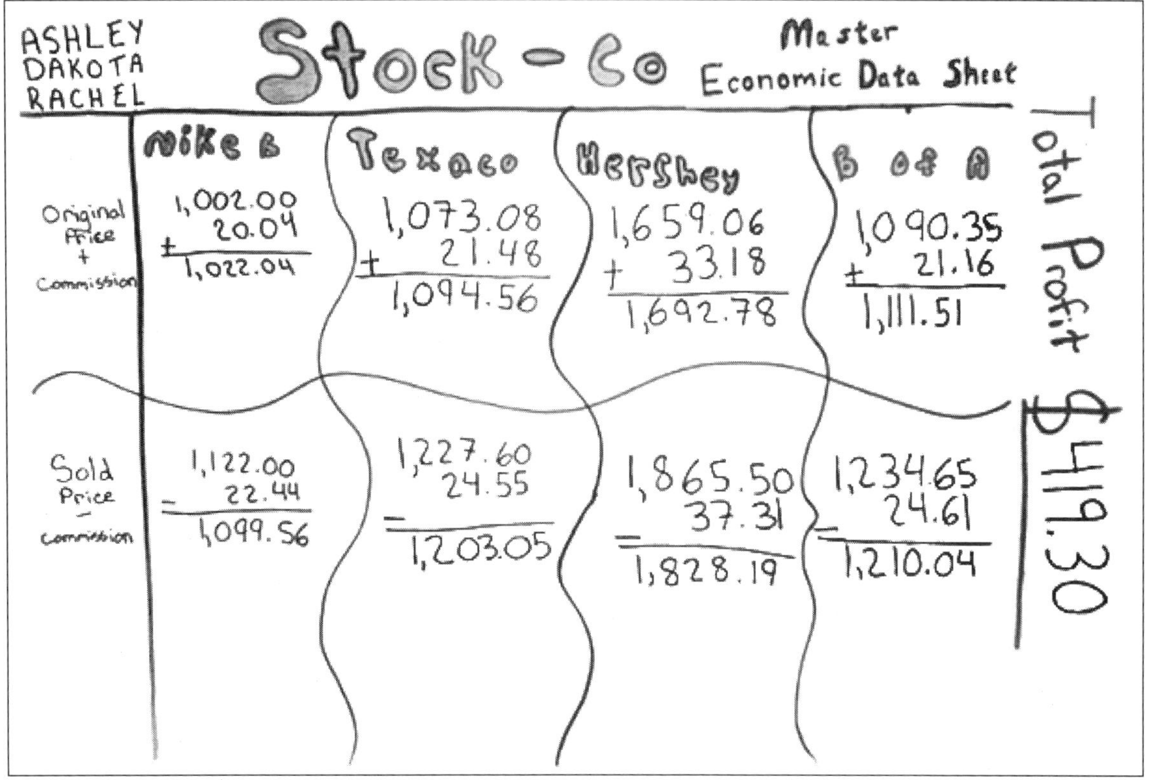

Selling Stock

Materials

- Several current copies of the *Wall Street Journal* or another newspaper that prints the stock tables
- Blackline Master: Order to Sell (1–2 per group)
- Overhead Transparency: Order to Sell

In this lesson, students will

- **learn the procedure for selling stock**
- **sell stock if they wish**
- **buy new stock to replace what they have sold**

Rethinking Investments

One day each week can be set aside for selling old stocks and buying new ones. If a particular stock is not doing well for an investment company, the students may decide to sell it and buy something else. A 2% broker's commission must be paid on all stock sold, and students will find that it can become costly to make changes in their investment portfolios. Students can always stay on the lookout for promising stocks to buy. You may wish to suggest that they choose some stocks to track without actually buying. This way, they may have some hot prospects lined up if they do decide to unload some of their purchases.

Order to Sell

Use the overhead projector to review the correct way to fill out an Order to Sell form. Be sure that students record the New Value of Stocks as a deposit (a credit) into their company checking account. Students must also write a check to the broker for the commission, and that amount must also be recorded, as a debit, in the checkbook register.

Choose a New Company

To replace stock which has been sold, simply repeat the process of choosing new stock and then filling out a Purchase Request. The purchase amount can be as much as the balance that the investment company has in its checking account. For example, if the company has a balance of $38.95 left over from its original purchases, this money can now be combined with the money from the sale of old stock to buy new.

If your brokerage firm has a checking account, you will write out a check to the investment company for the new value of the stock. Or simply record the deposit into the credit column of the company's checkbook register.

LESSON 8

Wrapping Up the Unit

In this lesson, students will complete a final activity (or several activities) which will bring this unit to a close

Materials

- Several current copies of the *Wall Street Journal* or another newspaper that prints the stock tables
- Miscellaneous materials, depending on the form of the final reports
- Blackline Master: Order to Sell (several per group)

Final Activity

Set a date for the last investment day of this simulation. An Order to Sell form must be completed on that day for every stock each company owns. The new value of each stock is recorded into the checking account as a credit. Checks are written to the broker for 2% of each sale and recorded as debits in the check registers. The final balance in the checking account, subtracted from $5,000.00, is the total profit or loss.

At this time you can have investment companies make their final reports. They may report their profits or, possibly, their losses. The final presentation can include both an oral and a written report. The portfolio should be well-organized and should contain job descriptions, buy and sell orders, checks and a check register, graphs, and all other materials. Assign the final activity based on your students' ages and abilities.

Elements to Consider for the Final Activity

The sample questions on page 24 can be assigned for student reports. Choose those you would like students to address. You can write the requirements for the report on the chalkboard, or use your overhead projector. It is up to you to decide on a written or oral format for reporting, or on both. You might base your decision on what to require for the final activity on factors such as how much time you wish to allot for student research, for student preparation of presentation materials, for listening to oral reports, and for your reading and evaluation of written work.

Suggested Questions and Items for Final Activities

Listed first are some sample questions to present to students, followed by a list of final activity features. Some of the features have been required activities in earlier lessons. For the final report, however, these graphs and charts, and so on, should be reworked to be of presentation quality. For example, if the presentation is oral, in front of the class, graphs and charts must be large enough to be read from the back of the room. If the final report is to be written and placed in a presentation folder, graphs and charts will have to be made to fit that format.

Sample Questions

- Which companies were chosen and why? (Investors may have chosen local businesses, "green" companies, technological firms, or simply familiar companies, such as McDonald's or Nike.)
- What happened with each stock over time? Students should display their results in line graphs.
- What was the group's thinking over time about selling the original stock and buying new?
- What kind of problems or disagreements, if any, did the group encounter? How were these problems resolved?
- What were the group's strengths?
- In your opinion, what should your group have done differently? The same? Why?

Final Activity Features

Background information about each of the companies in which students invested. If a prospectus from each company was sent for, (see Extensions, page x), these reports will be an excellent source of information.

Graphs clearly showing the progress of each stock over the time allowed. This visual information may be displayed attractively on a chalkboard or an overhead projection screen. (Check on the availability of color overheads.)

Charts clearly showing the amount of profit or loss for each stock. Remind students to include broker's commission payments somewhere in this information.

A master chart showing how much total money the investors earned or lost.

The company books (portfolio contents, including the checking account) made available for auditing).

A Self-Evaluation (see Blackline Master, page 31) completed by each investor.

A Group Evaluation (see Blackline Master, page 32) completed by each investor.

A final statement prepared by the company as to whether the investors would make the same stock choices again. Why or why not? What would they like to do differently (investment-wise) if they were to participate in this activity a second time?

APPENDIX

Assessment Tools

There are numerous methods by which to assess student work. The goal is to find out if students have learned what you had intended them to learn and to see if they picked up other information or skills beyond your expectations. Teachers have different preferences depending on personal style and grade level. With that in mind, this book includes a number of suggestions for assessment. Use any or all of the assessment ideas that will work well for you. On the following pages you will find the following assessment tools:

Rubrics 27

Blackline Master Forms 30

Simulation Tools

The tools provided for this simulation include reference materials and worksheets. Reference materials include Blackline Masters: Reading the NYSE, Simulation Guidelines, Job Descriptions, Glossary, and Parent Letter. The remaining Blackline Masters are worksheets students use to keep track of their bank accounts and other stock transactions. They can be made into overhead transparencies and used as instructional aids. Investment forms, containing sample data, are also provided for your information.

Blackline Masters (reference and worksheets) 33

Samples of Filled-In Investment Forms 48

RUBRIC FOR PORTFOLIOS

Points	Indicators
5	All of the paperwork is organized in a portfolio in a logical sequence and none is missing. This includes the checkbook register, cancelled checks, Purchase Requests, Track Records, Order to Sell forms, and Broker's Commission Report. Track Records are in chronological order. Paperwork has been filled out completely and is in students' best printing or handwriting. Final written report elements and research materials (if assigned) have been completed as instructed.
4	Paperwork in the portfolio shows some organizational plan. Track Records, specifically, have been accurately completed and are in chronological order. Other forms (checkbook register, cancelled checks Purchase Requests, Order to Sell forms, and Broker's Commission Report) may not be in an apparent logical order. Students have a good amount of work showing the research they have been conducting. The final written report (if assigned) is complete.
3	Paperwork in the portfolio shows evidence of an organizational plan. There may be some items missing, such as the checkbook register, cancelled checks Purchase Requests, Order to Sell forms, or the Broker's Commission Report. Track Records may not be in chronological order. The work may not be in the students' best printing or writing. There may be gaps in the report and research materials.
2	Portfolio lacks evidence of an organizational plan. Many of the required items are missing. The work that is present may be in haphazard condition. There is little evidence that students have conducted assigned research. Final report is incomplete.
1	Portfolio does not contain required elements, but some effort has been made.
0	No portfolio was submitted.

RUBRIC FOR ORAL REPORTS

Points	Indicators
5	The group made excellent use of visual aids to convey information. Everyone contributed to the report. The group presented their information clearly. The presentation clearly demonstrated that the students understood the process of buying, tracking, and selling stocks. All of the elements assigned in Lesson 8 for the oral report were addressed.
4	Visual aids were utilized. Most or all of the group members contributed to the report. Most of the information was explained in a way that could be understood. The students showed that they understood, and were able to effectively apply, the math concepts necessary to complete the activities. All or most of the elements assigned for the oral report were present.
3	Visual aids were used but did not have a clear connection to the content of the oral report. Or, visual aids were not of presentation quality. Information was not clearly organized. Some information was hard to follow. Students were able to apply the math concepts necessary to complete the activities. Some of the required elements assigned for the oral report were present.
2	Visual aids were not used or were not appropriate. Information was presented in a way that was unclear, incomplete or lacked reasoning. Students did not show that they understood the mathematics involved in the project. There were major gaps in the required elements of the report.
1	Visual aids were not used. The report did not contain the required elements, but some effort was made.
0	Report was not attempted by the group.

RUBRIC FOR JOURNALS

If you have chosen to have your students keep a journal (see Extensions, page x) either as a group or individually, you may opt to grade the journals on a 5-point scale. You may grade them by entry, or as a whole, at the end of the simulation. It's a good idea for students to keep a journal during the simulation. Writing about the process encourages students to organize their thoughts and, as a result, enhances their understanding. If you choose to review journals periodically, you will have the opportunity to assess their progress and provide intervention when necessary.

Most of the suggested journal topics might be used to help students process the day's activity. Others are intended to help students focus on what they need to do the next time their investment group meets. Some are designed to give students practice in a mathematical skill or procedure they have just learned by having them describe the steps involved. This 5-point scale is meant to give you a general idea of what you might look at when assessing a journal or a journal entry.

Points	Indicators
5	Outstanding written work. Explanations are clear and concise. Demonstrates a clear understanding of the mathematics required.
4	Good written work. Explanations are understandable. Shows an understanding of the mathematics required.
3	Satisfactory written work. Explanations are present. Most of the mathematics are understood, but there may be areas that are unclear or incomplete.
2	Weak written work. Explanations may be attempted but are unclear and incomplete. Student has not shown an understanding of the mathematics involved.
1	Unacceptable written work. Explanations are unclear or missing. Student has been unable to demonstrate an understanding of any of the mathematics required.
0	No journal was submitted.

TEACHER OBSERVATION SHEET

Date:

Student's Name: ______________________________

Activity: ______________________________

____

Accomplishes the Task: ______________________________

____

____

Demonstrates Organizational Skills: ______________________________

____

____

Communicates Effectively with Group Members: ______________________________

____

____

Uses Acceptable Mathematical Terminology: ______________________________

____

____

Is Able to Perform the Computations Necessary to the Task:

____

____

____

____

____

____

Rating

0 not observed

1 not able to perform this task

2 accomplishes with some difficulty

3 proficient in this area

4 shows strength in this area

SELF-EVALUATION

Investment Company: ______________________________

Name: ______________________________

Job Title: ______________________________

I made the following contributions to my group: ______________________________

____

____

____

I think my fellow group members would say that I: ______________________________

____

____

____

My best contribution was: ______________________________

____

____

____

I would change the following about the way I worked within my group: ______

____

____

____

GROUP EVALUATION

Investment Company: ______________________________

Name: ______________________________

Job Title: ______________________________

Discuss how well (or poorly) you believe your group members got along with each other. Give a specific example to support your opinion.

____

____

How did your group go about making decisions? What process was used to settle conflicting ideas?

____

____

What was the greatest strength of your group? What did you all do the best together?

____

____

What were the main problems your group ran into and how were they handled?

____

____

____

What have you learned about working in groups? What are some things that have to be done in order for a team to work successfully together?

____

____

____

READING THE NYSE

52-Week Hi/Lo

The 52-week high and low stock prices are displayed in the newspaper as the first two columns of numbers. These columns show the highest price and the lowest price each share has sold for during the past year. In most newspapers, the cents are given in fraction form, for example: $11\frac{3}{4}$ is equal to $11.75.

This information is useful to investors because they can compare it to the price a stock is selling for today and then try to predict what will happen to it in the near future. For example: let's say a stock had a high of $55.00 per share and a low of $22.00. Today, that stock is selling for $53.00. What can you predict from this information? Do you suppose that the value has been increasing over the past year? What if that same stock today costs $23.00? Do you suppose the value of that stock is dropping?

Stock

The third column in the table lists the company name and the type of stock. The type of stock is indicated by abbreviations immediately following the name, such as "pf," "wt," "rt," "un," or "wi." If no abbreviations appear after the name, the stock is referred to as "common." The abbreviations pertain to such things as distribution of dividends, rights to buy at certain prices and in certain amounts, and whether the stock must be bought as a "package deal." For this unit, choose only common stocks.

Sym

Each stock has a unique symbol. This symbol is used to identify the stock on electronic systems, databases, and the stock exchange ticker. If you want to locate your stock on the Internet, it will be helpful to know the stock symbol. You may also use the company stock symbol as an abbreviation when filling out Order to Buy, Order to Sell, or Track Record forms during this unit.

Div

A dividend is a sum of money paid to shareholders out of a company's earnings. The dividend column of the stock table shows the amount that was paid out per share of stock during the preceding 52 weeks. Dividend payments are a sign of how well a company is doing. Stable companies that believe they can predict what their profits are going to be, usually pay out higher dividends. The actual amount that will be paid out in dividends is decided upon by the board of directors of a particular company. The payment and collection of dividends are not part of this unit, but your investment group may want to take dividend payments into consideration as they are choosing stock.

Yld %

The Percent Yield is calculated by dividing the dividend payment by the day's closing price. This figure is *supposed* to represent what an investor can expect to get back in a dividend payment.

PE

The Price/Earnings ratio (PE) is another figure used to predict how a stock may be expected to perform. An investor would divide the closing price (close) by the figure provided in the PE column. The *quotient* (the number you get when you divide one number into another) gives you the earnings per share for the past year. There can be many factors contributing to a high or low P/E ratio. Unless the investor does some research into the prospective company, it isn't recommended to use a high or low P/E ratio as an indicator of whether the stock value will increase.

Vol 100s

"Volume 100s" refers to the number of shares traded (bought and sold) on a given day. The figure must be multiplied by 100 to give the actual number of shares traded. For example, if a company's "Vol 100s" figure is 693, the number of shares traded was 69,300. If a "z" appears before the figure, then the number represents the *actual* number of shares traded and should not be multiplied by 100. For example, z24 would mean that only 24 shares of that stock were traded. If an underline appears across the columns of information for a particular stock, it means that an unusually high amount of that stock was traded for the day.

Hi Lo

The next two columns are the high and low sales prices for just that day. These figures tell investors how much the price changed. If the high or low is a new record for that stock, an up or down arrow is printed to the far left of the listing. A company's stock hitting a low can be bad news if you have already bought it. Then again, it could be a good time to "buy in" if you have reason to believe the price will begin to rise again.

READING THE NYSE, cont.

Close or Last

This column is very important for this unit. The number in this column shows how much a stock was finally sold for when the stock exchange closed down on the previous day. When investors choose the stocks they are going to buy, this is the column they will look at to see how much they will have to pay. When investors are ready to sell stock, this column will show the amount of money they will be paid per share owned. Again, the cent amounts are sometimes shown in fraction form. If you're looking at Tuesday's newspaper, the close listed would be Monday's closing price (unless Monday was a holiday, in which case the stock exchange would have been closed).

Net Chg

The net change is calculated by subtracting the currently listed closing price from the previous day's closing price. If the stock value has risen since the day before, a plus sign (+) will appear before the dollar amount (frequently shown as a fraction of a dollar). If the stock closed at a lower price, a minus sign (–) will appear. If there is no entry in the net change column, then there has been no change from the previous day. If the listing is in boldface, it means the Close is either up or down more than 5% from the day before.

CONVERTING FRACTIONS TO DECIMALS

A fraction can be thought of as a division problem. The common fraction 3/4, for example, can be read "3 divided by 4." Using a calculator, we can get the decimal equivalent quickly and easily: 3 divided by 4 is equal to 0.75.

Fraction	Convert to decimal	Round (if necessary); Show as dollar amount
3/4	0.75	$ 0.75
5/8	0.625	$ 0.63
1/8		
7/8		
1/4		
1/2		
3/8		
1 5/8		
1 1/4		
1 3/8		
1 1/8		

When you begin to calculate the price of stock, you may want to refer back to these fraction-to-dollar amounts.

SIMULATION GUIDELINES

1. Each group will receive $5,000.00 to invest in the stock market.

2. Investors must spend a minimum of $4,900.00 on stocks and broker's commissions but may not exceed the $5,000.00 limit. Leftover funds will be kept in the investment company checking account for possible later use. (It probably won't be possible for investors to reach the exact $5,000.00 amount.)

3. Each group must choose at least three but no more than five companies from which to purchase stock.

4. A 2% commission must be paid to the stockbroker for every stock bought and for every stock sold.

5. Every group is responsible for keeping track records for each stock it owns. These records, and all other stock records, will be kept in the investment portfolio.

6. Periodically, the total profit or loss will be recorded onto a master economic data sheet.

7. A final activity will be completed by all investment groups as assigned.

JOB DESCRIPTIONS

Purchasing Agent

Responsible for filling out all paperwork regarding the buying and selling of stocks, including Purchase Requests, Order to Sell forms, and Track Records.

Runner

Responsible for out-of-seat duties, such as taking Stock Purchase Requests to the broker, recording information on classroom economic data sheets, and picking up supplies. The runner also supervises the construction of graphs showing profits and losses.

Accountant

Checks all of the math figures made by the Purchasing Agent, and keeps track of broker's commissions. The accountant also manages the bank account, and writes and signs checks.

Operations Manager

Keeps the Track Records, and organizes the portfolio. The Operations Manager is also responsible for leading the group meetings.

PURCHASE REQUEST

Stock Name: ______________________________

Date from Newspaper: ______________________________

Investment Company: ______________________________

Closing price from newspaper: ______________

How many shares do you want to buy? ______________

Multiply to get cost of shares: ______________

Enter cost of shares again: ______________

Calculate the broker's commission by multiplying cost of shares by .02 (or 2%) ______________

(If necessary, round this figure to the nearest hundredth. Then write a check for this amount and enter it on the Broker's Commission Report.)

Purchasing Agent's Initials: ________

Accountant's Initials: ________

Broker's Stamp of Approval

CHECKBOOK REGISTER

Number	Date	Description of Transaction	Payment (Debit)	Deposit (Credit)	Balance $

CHECKS

CHECK NO. ____________

DATE ____________

PAY TO THE ORDER OF ____

____ DOLLARS $ ____________

____
AUTHORIZED SIGNATURE

____
MEMO ____________________ INVESTMENT COMPANY

CHECK NO. ____________

DATE ____________

PAY TO THE ORDER OF ____

____ DOLLARS $ ____________

____
AUTHORIZED SIGNATURE

____
MEMO ____________________ INVESTMENT COMPANY

CHECK NO. ____________

DATE ____________

PAY TO THE ORDER OF ____

____ DOLLARS $ ____________

____
AUTHORIZED SIGNATURE

____
MEMO ____________________ INVESTMENT COMPANY

BROKER'S COMMISSION REPORT

Investment Company ____________________

Stock Name	Buying or Selling	Check Number	Broker's Commission

Total Broker's Commissions ____________

ORDER TO SELL

Investment Company: ______________________________

Date from Newspaper: ______________________________

Stock Name: ______________________________

New Closing Price: ______________________________

× Number of Shares Owned ______________________________

= New Value of Stocks ______________________________

Calculate the Broker's Commission:

Enter New Value of Stocks ______________________________

Enter Broker's Commission (× 2%) ______________________________

Enter on Broker's Commission Sheet ______________________________

New Value ______________________________

Minus Broker's Commission ______________________________

= Amount you will receive from broker ______________________________

Subtract Original Cost of Shares ______________________________
(from Purchase Request)

= Profit or Loss from Sale ______________________________

TRACK RECORD

Fill in the top portion of this Track Record with your original purchasing information for one of your stocks. This information will remain the same from one Track Record to the next. The New Information portion below will change each time you check the stock listing.

Original Information

Stock Name ______________________ Date Purchased ____________

$ ______________ × ______________ = $ ______________

Buy-In Price # of Shares Original Net Value

New Information

Date from Newspaper ______________

$ ______________ × ______________ = $ ______________

Closing Price # of Shares New Net Value

New Net Value ______________

– Original Net Value ______________

____

Is this figure positive or negative? If it is positive, this would be the profit you would make if you were to sell your shares today. If it is negative, it represents the money you would lose if you were to sell your shares today.

Investment Company ______________________________

$ ______________ Profit or Loss? (circle one)

Operations Manager's Initials __________ Accountant's Initials __________

GLOSSARY

Most of the words listed in this glossary have many definitions. The definitions here reflect the usage within the context of this book.

A

auditor One of the teacher's roles. The person authorized to inspect accounting records.

B

broker One of the teacher's roles. An agent who buys or sells stock on a commission basis.

brokerage house The place of business for a broker.

C

cancel To stamp a check to show that it has been processed by a bank.

close The last price a particular stock sold for at the end of the business day.

commission A sum or percentage allowed in a business transaction. In this unit, 2% of the gross sale.

credit A deposit amount made to the checking account. A positive figure.

D

debit An amount drawn against the checking account. A negative figure.

dividend A sum of money paid to shareholders.

Dow Jones Average The oldest continuous price index of the stock market. Named after newsman Charles Henry Dow. A tool invented to help analyze the stock market's ups and downs.

G

green companies Businesses publicly committed to activities not harmful to the environment.

H

hundredth The position of the second digit to the right of the decimal point.

I

index An indicator.

indicator A sign of. Something which implies.

L

loss Opposite of profit. What happens when you sell stock for less than you paid for it.

M

market The New York Stock Exchange.

marketplace The world of commerce.

N

NYSE Abbreviation for the New York Stock Exchange.

O

Order to Sell A form in this unit used to record the final selling price of a stock and to calculate the profit or loss on that sale.

P

portfolio A folder containing the paperwork for this unit. The stocks and bonds owned by a person for investment purposes.

price earnings ratio The ratio of the market price of a share of common stock to the earnings per share.

profit Earnings that accrue when you sell stock at a higher price than you paid for it.

prospectus A report describing a company.

Purchase Request A form in this unit used to indicate which stock an investment company wishes to purchase. Useful in calculating the cost of shares and the broker's commission.

Q

quotation The current market price of a stock as listed in the NYSE Composite Transactions.

quotient The result of division.

S

stock The outstanding capital of a company or corporation. The shares of a particular company or corporation.

stockbroker A person who buys and sells stocks for his or her customers.

T

thousandths The position of the third digit to the right of the decimal point.

track To monitor the progress of a particular stock.

Track Record A form in this unit used to record periodically the closing price of a particular stock.

trade The act of buying and selling.

V

value The monetary worth of something.

Y

yield To earn a profit.

yield percent Calculated by dividing the dividend payment (Div.) by the closing price (Close).

PARENT LETTER

Date:

Dear Parent,

During the next few weeks your student will be participating in a stock market simulation game. In this simulation, students will learn how to read the stock market pages, “buy” stocks, and monitor the progress of their investments.

This simulation is set up as a game. Your student will be assigned to an investment group. Each group will have an imaginary $5,000.00 to spend on stocks and broker’s commissions. The groups will be in competition with each other to see who can earn the largest profit in the time allowed. Over the course of the simulation, investment groups will have the option to sell stocks and choose new ones to purchase. Along the way, investment groups will be researching the companies in which they are interested and will prepare a final project to present to the class.

While participating in this stock market simulation, students will apply many of the math skills they have been learning in class, including organizing information, graphing, basic accounting, working with decimal numbers, finding percents, converting fractions to decimals, problem solving, and critical thinking. Students will also use the Internet to conduct research and practice decision making.

Please encourage your student to share his or her experiences and thoughts with you during the simulation. Also, feel free to visit our classroom and observe your student’s involvement in the activities. Please contact me with any questions you may have.

Sincerely,

PURCHASE REQUEST SAMPLE

Stock Name: Nike B

Date from Newspaper: February 10, 1998

Investment Company: Stock Co.

Closing price from newspaper: $41.75

How many shares do you want to buy? 24

Multiply to get cost of shares: $41.75 x 24 = $1,002.00

Enter cost of shares again: $1,002.00

Calculate the broker's commission by multiplying cost of shares by .02 (or 2%) $1,002.00 x .02 = $20.04

(If necessary, round this figure to the nearest hundredth. Then write a check for this amount and enter it on the Broker's Commission Report.)

Purchasing Agent's Initials: _______

Accountant's Initials: _______

Broker's Stamp of Approval

CHECKBOOK REGISTER SAMPLE

Number	Date	Description of Transaction	Payment (Debit)	√	Deposit (Credit)	Balance $5,000.00
0001	2/10/98	Acme Brokerage	96.51			
		Payment of Commissions				4,903.49
0002	2/10/98	Acme Brokerage	4,825.21			
		Stock Purchases				78.28

CHECKS SAMPLES

CHECK NO. 0001

DATE 2/10/98

PAY TO THE ORDER OF Acme Brokerage House

Ninety Six 51/100 DOLLARS $ 96.51

Ms./Mr. Accountant
AUTHORIZED SIGNATURE

Stock Co.
INVESTMENT COMPANY

MEMO Commissions

CHECK NO. 0002

DATE 2/10/98

PAY TO THE ORDER OF Acme Brokerage House

Four thousand eight hundred twenty-five 21/100 DOLLARS $ 4,825.21

Ms./Mr. Accountant
AUTHORIZED SIGNATURE

Stock Co.
INVESTMENT COMPANY

MEMO Stock Purchases

BROKER'S COMMISSION REPORT SAMPLE

Investment Company	Stock Name	Buying or Selling	Check Number	Broker's Commission
Stock Co.	Nike B	buying	0001	$20.04
	Texaco	buying	0002	21.48
	Hershey	buying	0003	33.18
	B of A	buying	0004	21.16
	Nike B	selling	——	22.44
	Texaco	selling	——	24.55
	Hershey	selling	——	37.31
	B of A	selling	——	24.61

Total Broker's Commissions ____________________

ORDER TO SELL SAMPLE

Investment Company: Stock Co.

Date from Newspaper: 4/2/98

Stock Name: Nike B

New Closing Price: $46.75

× Number of Shares Owned $46.75 x 24 = $1,122.00

= New Value of Stocks $1,122.00

Calculate the Broker's Commission:

Enter New Value of Stocks $1,122.00

Enter Broker's Commission (× 2%) $1,122.00 x .02 = $22.44

Enter on Broker's Commission Sheet $22.44

New Value $1,122.00

Minus Broker's Commission $1,122.00 – $22.44 = $1,099.56

= Amount you will receive from broker $1,099.56

Subtract Original Cost of Shares + Commission $1,022.04
(from Purchase Request)
= (Profit) or Loss from Sale $77.52

TRACK RECORD SAMPLE

Fill in the top portion of this Track Record with your original purchasing information for one of your stocks. This information will remain the same from one track record to the next. The New Information portion below will change each time you check the stock listing.

Original Information

Stock Name Nike B   Date Purchased 2/10/98

$ 41.75 × 24 = $ 1,002.00

Buy-In Price   # of Shares   Original Net Value

New Information

Date from Newspaper 3/19/98

$ 46.08 × 24 = $ 1,105.92

Closing Price   # of Shares   New Net Value

New Net Value $1,105.92

– Original Net Value $1,002.00

$103.92

Is this figure positive or negative? If it is positive, this would be the profit you would make if you were to sell your shares today. If it is negative, it represents the money you would lose if you were to sell your shares today.

Investment Company Stock Co.

$ 103.92 (Profit circled) or Loss? (circle one)

Operations Manager's Initials ________ Accountant's Initials ________